Cardiac Diet

The Ultimate Guide for Healthy Living

Author

Chrissy M. Winchester

Contents

THE PLANT-BASED CARDIAC DIET

THE PLANT-BASED CARDIAC DIET

What if one simple change could put you on a path to better health? And what if that change could even save you from Heart Problem? You have the power to transform your life by maintaining a plant-based diet - no ifs about it. It's a sure path to your healthy recovery.

While many omnivores feel that a meal without meat just doesn't feel like a meal, the vegan and vegetarian plant- based lifestyle is growing in popularity just the same - and with good reason. A plant-based diet moves away from animal-based foods like meat, eggs, and milk, and incorporates more fruit, vegetables, legumes, and grains. The less meat and dairy you eat the less fat you take in. This goes a long way when it comes to maintaining healthy living and lifestyle.

If you're wondering whether you should try out a plant- based diet, consider the top benefits it provides for your overall health. Keep in mind that you don't have to jump into a full-on vegan diet or vegetarian diet. Just limit your

intake of meat, poultry, and dairy, and increasing vegetables, fruit, and grains can do wonders for your health.

I have included in this book, healthy and delicious recipes for your daily consumptions. These recipes have been tested to have a positive impact on your recovery process.

PLANT-BASED CARDIAC DIET RECIPES

1. Hearty Vegetarian Baked Beans

Prep Time: 10 mins Cook Time: 10 mins Total Time: 20 mins

Servings: 6

Ingredients

• 1 (12 ounce) package Impossible Burger • ½ medium onion, chopped • ½ teaspoon garlic salt • ¼ teaspoon ground black pepper • 1 (22 ounce) can baked beans • 4 tablespoons ketchup • 1 teaspoon prepared yellow mustard • 3 tablespoons honey

• ½ teaspoon white vinegar Directions

1. Combine meatless ground beef, onion, garlic salt, and pepper in a pot over medium to medium-high heat. Cook and stir until browned, about 5 minutes.

2. Add baked beans, ketchup, mustard, honey, and vinegar; stir until completely combined and heated through, about 5 minutes more. Serve warm.

2. Vegetarian Taco-Stuffed Peppers

Prep Time: 20 mins Cook Time: 30 mins Total Time: 50 mins

Servings: 3

Ingredients

• 1 medium red bell pepper • 1 medium yellow bell pepper • 1 medium orange bell pepper • 2 tablespoons olive oil • 1 (12 ounce) package Impossible Burger • 1 small onion, minced • 2 cloves garlic, minced • 1 (1 ounce) envelope taco seasoning mix

• 1 (14.5 ounce) can fire-roasted diced tomatoes • 1 ½ cups shredded Mexican blend cheese, divided

- ¼ cup minced fresh cilantro • ¾ cup sour cream

- ¾ cup prepared guacamole

Directions

1. Preheat the oven to 375 degrees F (190 degrees C).

2. Cut bell peppers in half vertically through the stem and remove the seeds. Place cut-sides down in a baking dish to allow excess moisture to drain.

3. Bake in the preheated oven for 10 minutes. Remove from the oven, flip peppers over, cut-sides up, and set aside.

4. Heat oil in a large skillet over medium-high heat. Cook meatless ground beef and onion in the hot pan, breaking up any large pieces, until browned, 5 to 6 minutes.

5. Add garlic and stir until cooked through, about 2 minutes more. Sprinkle with taco seasoning and stir

in diced tomatoes until combined. Stir in 3/4 cup Mexican cheese.

6. Stuff peppers with mixture and cover dish with foil.

7. Bake in the preheated oven until peppers are tender, 10 to 15 minutes. Remove foil and top peppers with remaining cheese. Return to the oven and bake until cheese is melted, 2 to 3 minutes.

8. Sprinkle with cilantro and serve each pepper with a dollop of sour cream and guacamole.

3. World's Best (Now Vegetarian!) Lasagna Prep Time: 30 mins

Cook Time: 2 hrs 30 mins

Total Time: 3 hrs 15 mins

Servings: 12

Ingredients

• 1 tablespoon olive oil • ½ cup minced onion • 2 cloves garlic, crushed • 8 ounces plant-based hot Italian-style sausage (such as Beyond Meat), chopped • 6 ounces cooked and crumbled ground meat substitute (such as BOCA) • 1 (15 ounce) can crushed tomatoes • 1 (8 ounce) can tomato sauce • 1 (6 ounce) can tomato paste • ¼ cup water

• 3 tablespoons chopped fresh parsley, divided • 1 tablespoon white sugar • ¾ teaspoon dried basil • 1 teaspoon salt, divided • ½ teaspoon Italian seasoning • ¼ teaspoon fennel seeds • ⅛ teaspoon ground black pepper • 12 lasagna noodles • 1 egg, lightly beaten • 1 (15 ounce) container ricotta cheese • 12 ounces mozzarella cheese, sliced • 6 ounces grated Parmesan cheese

Directions

1. Heat oil in a Dutch oven over medium heat. Add onion and garlic; cook, stirring, until tender, 3 to 5 minutes.

2. Stir in plant-based sausage, meat substitute crumbles, crushed tomatoes, tomato sauce, tomato paste, water, 1 tablespoon parsley, sugar, basil, 1/2 teaspoon salt, Italian seasoning, fennel seeds, and pepper.

3. Bring to a boil; reduce heat and simmer, covered, stirring occasionally, until thickened, about 1 1/2 hours.

4. Bring a large pot of lightly salted water to a boil. Add lasagna noodles; cook 8 to 10 minutes. Drain and rinse noodles with cold water.

5. Preheat the oven to 375 degrees F (190 degrees C).

6. Meanwhile, stir together egg, ricotta, remaining 2 tablespoons parsley, and 1/2 teaspoon salt in a bowl.

7. To assemble lasagna, spread 1/3 of the sauce in a 9x13-inch baking dish. Arrange 6 noodles lengthwise over sauce.

8. Spread with 1/2 of the ricotta mixture. Top with 1/3 of the mozzarella slices. Spoon 1/3 of the sauce over

mozzarella and sprinkle with 1/4 cup Parmesan. Repeat layers and top with remaining mozzarella and Parmesan.

9. Bake, covered with cooking spray-coated foil, for 25 minutes. Remove foil and bake until hot and bubbly, about 25 minutes more. Cool for 15 minutes before slicing into 12 equal servings.

4. Beef Vegan Meatballs

Prep Time: 25 mins Cook Time: 1 hr

Total Time: 1 hr 25 mins

Servings: 8

Ingredients

• 1 (10 ounce) package frozen chopped spinach • 2 tablespoons water • 2 (16 ounce) packages Beyond Meat Beyond Beef plant-based ground • ¾ cup nutritional yeast • ¾ cup vegan bread crumbs (such as Aleia's) • 4 tablespoons tomato paste • 5 cloves garlic, minced • 1 tablespoon dried oregano leaves • 1 tablespoon dried basil leaves

• 1 teaspoon onion powder • ½ teaspoon salt • ½ teaspoon ground black pepper • 4 tablespoons olive oil, divided, or more as needed

Directions

1. Combine frozen spinach and water in a 1-quart microwave-safe casserole dish. Cover and microwave on high for 5 minutes, stirring halfway through the cooking time.

2. Break up any clumps with a fork and cook for 1 more minute.

3. Transfer to a colander to drain. When cool enough to handle, squeeze small handfuls of spinach to release remaining water and place spinach in a large mixing bowl.

4. Add Beyond Beef, nutritional yeast, bread crumbs, tomato paste, minced garlic, oregano, basil, onion powder, salt, and pepper to the spinach.

5. Mix with your hands until all ingredients are thoroughly combined. Roll into 1 1/4-inch diameter meatballs.

6. Preheat oven to 400 degrees F (200 degrees C). Line a large rimmed baking sheet with parchment paper.

7. Heat 1 tablespoon olive oil over medium heat in a large Dutch oven.

8. Working in batches, add about 12 meatballs and cook, turning often and being careful not to burn, until browned on all sides, about 5 to 7 minutes.

9. Transfer meatballs to the prepared baking sheet, and repeat with remaining batches.

10. Bake in the preheated oven until heated through, 30 to 35 minutes.

11. An instant-read thermometer inserted into the center should read at least 165 degrees F (74 degrees

5. Heart Beet Vegetable Burgers

Prep Time: 30 mins Cook Time: 20 mins Total Time: 50 mins

Servings: 10

Ingredients

- 2 ½ cooked, mashed sweet potatoes

- 1 ½ cups quinoa, cooked and cooled

- a third of a cup of trail mix

- 12 cup whole wheat flour • 12 cup whole wheat bread crumbs • 13 cup olive oil • 12 red onion, chopped • 5 tablespoons parsley, minced • 3 teaspoons tamari • 1 big golden beet, grated

12 teaspoon red pepper flakes • 1 tablespoon sea salt • 4 garlic cloves, chopped

Directions

1. Preheat the oven to 350 degrees Fahrenheit (175 degrees C). A baking sheet should be greased.

2. In a large mixing bowl, combine sweet potatoes, quinoa, trail mix, golden and red beets, flour, bread crumbs, oil, onion, parsley, tamari, sea salt, garlic, and red pepper flakes. Hand-mix the burger mix until it is well incorporated.

3. Divide the burger mixture into ten pieces and shape each one into a patty. Place on the baking sheet that has been prepared.

4. Bake for 20 minutes in a preheated oven until golden brown.

6. Black Bean and Corn Burgers with a Spicy Kick

15-minute prep time Time to prepare: 20 minutes Time allotted: 35 minutes 4 servings

Ingredients

1 tablespoon olive oil • 1 small onion, diced • 2 garlic cloves, minced • 1 jalapeno pepper, seeded and minced • 1 teaspoon dried oregano • 12 red bell pepper, diced • 1 ear corn, kernels cut from cob • 1 (15 ounce) can black beans, drained and rinsed • 12 cup plain bread crumbs • 4 teaspoons chili powder

• 12 teaspoon cumin • 12 teaspoon salt • 12 cup all-purpose flour, or as required • 1 tablespoon olive oil Directions

1. In a pan over medium heat, heat 1 tablespoon olive oil; sauté and stir onion, garlic, jalapeño pepper, and oregano until onions are translucent, about 8 to 10 minutes.

2. Cook and toss the red bell pepper and corn into the onion mixture for another 2 to 4 minutes, or until the red bell pepper is soft.

3. In a large mixing basin, mash black beans. In a mixing bowl, combine the vegetable mixture, bread crumbs, chili powder, cilantro, cumin, and salt. Coat both sides of each burger with flour after dividing the mixture into 4 patties.

4. In a pan over medium heat, heat 1 tablespoon olive oil; cook patties until browned, 5 to 8 minutes on each side.

7. Sweet Potato Burgers from North Africa

Time to Prepare: 30 minutes 30 minutes to prepare Servings: 8

Total Time: 1 hour

Ingredients

• 2 cups cooked and mashed sweet potatoes • 1 cup fast cooking oats • 34 cup chopped onion • 12 cup chopped peanuts • 12 cup chopped cilantro • 2 tablespoons minced fresh ginger • 2 garlic cloves, minced • 12 teaspoons cumin • 1 teaspoon salt

Directions

1. Preheat the oven to 350 degrees Fahrenheit (175 degrees C). Use vegetable oil to grease a 9x13-inch baking pan.

2. In a mixing dish, combine sweet potatoes, oats, onion, peanuts, cilantro, ginger, garlic, cumin, and salt. Mix until everything is well blended. Form the mixture into patties and place them on the baking sheet that has been prepared.

3. Bake for 15 minutes in a preheated oven until one side is browned. Bake until the opposite side of the patties is browned, approximately 15 minutes longer.

Prep Time: 1 Hour 8. Carrot Rice Nut Burger

1 hour 30 minutes to cook

2 hours 30 minutes total time

20 servings

Ingredients

- 1 cup roasted cashews • 1 pound toasted unsalted sunflower seeds

- 3 cups uncooked brown rice • 6 cups water

- 1 chopped sweet onion • 6 carrots • 1 tablespoon extra virgin olive oil • salt to taste

Directions

1. Bring the rice and water to a boil in a big saucepan. Reduce to a low heat setting, cover, and cook for 45 minutes.

2. Prepare the grill for high heat by preheating it.

3. Grind the roasted cashews and sunflower seeds to a fine meal in a food processor.

4. Transfer to a large mixing basin. In a food processor, coarsely shred the onion and carrots, then combine with the ground nuts.

5. In a food processor, combine the cooked rice and olive oil and pulse until smooth. Combine all ingredients in a mixing bowl. Season with salt and pepper. Make patties out of the mixture.

6. Brush the grill grate with oil. The patties should be grilled for 6 to 8 minutes on each side, or until beautifully browned.

Falafel Burgers (nine)

Time to Prepare: 20 minutes 15 minutes to prepare Time allotted: 35 minutes 4 servings

Ingredients

• 2 tablespoons olive oil, divided • 1 small red onion, diced • 1 big garlic clove, minced • 1 (16 ounce) can garbanzo beans (chickpeas), drained and washed • 1 (7.75 ounce) can spinach, thoroughly drained

Directions

1. Cook red onion and garlic in 1 tablespoon heated olive oil in a 12-inch skillet over medium heat for 5 minutes, or until tender-crisp.

2. Add one-fourth of the garbanzo beans, lemon juice, and salt to a food processor; pulse canned spinach until it forms a smooth puree.

3. Pulse in the rest of the garbanzo beans, breadcrumbs, and onion mixture until finely chopped.

4. Form the mixture into four 4-inch patties with your hands. (Refrigerate until ready to cook, if preferred.) Cook falafel patties in remaining tablespoon heated olive oil in 12-inch pan over medium heat until brown and crisp, rotating once. Serve with any of the above-mentioned accompaniments.

10. Black Bean Vegan Burgers

15-minute prep time Time to prepare: 20 minutes Time allotted: 35

minutes 4 servings

Ingredients

• 13 cup chopped sweet onion • 1 tablespoon minced garlic • 3

baby carrots, grated (optional) • 14 cup minced green bell pepper

(Optional)

• 1 teaspoon chili powder • 1 tablespoon cornstarch • 1 tablespoon

warm water • 3 tablespoons chile-garlic sauce (such as Sriracha®),

or to taste

• 1 teaspoon ground cumin • 1 teaspoon seafood seasoning (such as Old Bay) • 14 teaspoon salt • 14 teaspoon crushed black pepper • 2 slices whole-wheat bread, cut into little crumbs

Directions

1. Preheat the oven to 350 degrees Fahrenheit (175 degrees C). A baking sheet should be greased.

2. In a mixing bowl, mash black beans with onion, garlic, carrots, and green bell pepper. Mix.

3. In a separate small bowl, combine cornstarch, water, chile-garlic sauce, chili powder, cumin, seafood seasoning, salt, and black

pepper. Combine cornstarch and black bean mixture in a mixing bowl.

4. Toss in the whole-wheat bread with the bean mixture. 1/4 cup flour at a time, stir flour into bean mixture until a sticky dough forms.

5. Spoon burger-sized mounds of batter onto the prepared baking sheet, each approximately 3/4-inch thick. Make burgers out of the mixture.

6. Bake for 10 minutes on each side in a preheated oven until cooked in the middle and crisp on the exterior.

Prep time for the All-Star Veggie Burger is 20 minutes. Time to prepare: 10 minutes Time allotted: 30 minutes 8 servings

Ingredients

• 1 (15.5 ounce) can drained and mashed garbanzo beans • 8 chopped fresh basil leaves • 14 cup oat bran • 14 cup fast cooking oats • 1 cup cooked brown rice • 1 (14 ounce) package firm tofu • 5 teaspoons Korean barbecue sauce

• 12 tsp. salt • 12 tsp. crushed black pepper • 34 tsp. garlic powder

Directions: • 34 teaspoon dried sage • 2 tablespoons vegetable oil

1. Combine the mashed garbanzo beans and basil in a large mixing dish. Combine the oat bran, quick oats, and rice in a mixing bowl; the mixture should be somewhat dry.

2. Mash the tofu with your hands in a separate dish, squeezing out as much water as possible.

3. Drain the water and repeat the procedure until there isn't much left to drain out. The water does not have to be completely removed. Stir the barbecue sauce into the tofu to coat it.

4. Combine the tofu, garbanzo beans, and oats in a mixing bowl. Mix in the salt, pepper, garlic powder, and sage until everything is thoroughly combined.

5. In a large skillet, heat the oil over medium-high heat. Make patties with the bean mixture and fry them.

Cook for approximately 5 minutes each side in heated oil. Serve with burger buns.

Burgers with Kidney Beans and Black Thai Rice

15-minute prep time 1 hour 36 minutes to cook

2 hour total time 1 minute

8 servings

Ingredients

1 cup Thai black sticky rice • 2 14 cup water • 1 tablespoon olive oil • 1 red onion, diced • 2 garlic cloves, minced — 1 (14 ounce) can kidney beans, drained • 1 teaspoon chile powder • 1 teaspoon powdered paprika • 1 teaspoon ground turmeric • 2 tablespoons ketchup

• 1 CUP OF BAKED BREAD CRUMBS

• a third of a cup of essential wheat gluten

Directions

1. In a large pot, combine black rice and water. Bring the water to a boil. Cover, decrease heat, and cook for 45 to 50 minutes, or until rice is soft. Remove the pan from the heat. Cover and set aside for 10 minutes. Set aside 3 cups of the mixture after gently stirring it.

2. In a large skillet, heat the oil over medium heat. Cook, stirring often, until the onion is transparent, approximately 5 minutes. Cook and stir for 1 minute, or until garlic is golden. Remove the pan from the heat.

3. Preheat the oven to 375 degrees Fahrenheit (190 degrees C). A baking sheet should be greased.

4. In a large mixing basin, mash kidney beans until smooth. Add 3 cups cooked black rice, onion and garlic combination, chili powder, paprika, turmeric, ketchup, nutritional yeast, bread crumbs, and vital wheat to a large mixing bowl.

gluten, stirring well with a spoon or your hands after each addition until the mixture has the consistency of soft dough. Form 8 patties and place on a baking pan.

5. Bake patties for 20 minutes in a preheated oven until golden. Cook, flipping patties halfway through, until the second side is browned, approximately 20 minutes longer.

13. Delectable Portobello Mushroom Burgers

15-minute prep time Time to prepare: 10 minutes Time allotted: 35 minutes 4 servings

Ingredients

- 2 tbsp. olive oil • 2 tbsp. balsamic vinegar • 1 tbsp. Dijon mustard

- 2 chopped garlic cloves • 12 tbsp. Worcestershire sauce (Optional)

- 1 tsp. black pepper and 1 tsp. salt

- 4 kaiser rolls, divided • 4 big portobello mushrooms, stems removed

Directions

1. Lightly oil the grill grate and preheat the grill to medium-high heat.

2. In a mixing bowl, combine the olive oil, balsamic vinegar, Dijon mustard, garlic, Worcestershire sauce, salt, and pepper.

3. Brush the mixture over the mushrooms' tops and bottoms and set aside for 10 minutes.

4. Cook mushrooms on a hot grill with the lid covered for approximately 10 minutes, flipping once, until browned and tender. On kaiser rolls, serve.

8. Servings: 14 Mexican Bean Burgers

Ingredients

• 1 sliced carrot • 1 (15 ounce) can kidney beans • 12 cup chopped green bell pepper • 12 cup chopped onion • 2 cups salsa • 1 cup dry bread crumbs • 12 cup whole wheat flour • 12 teaspoon crushed black pepper • salt to taste Directions

1. Place the carrot in a bowl with approximately 1/4 inch of water in it. Cover with plastic wrap and heat for 2 minutes in the microwave, or until soft. Drain.

2. In a large mixing basin, mash the beans with the cooked carrot. Green pepper, onion, salsa, bread crumbs, and whole wheat flour should all be combined.

3. Add salt, black pepper, and chili powder to taste. If the mixture is too stiff, add additional salsa or flour to make it firmer. Make 8 patties out of the mixture and set them on a prepared baking pan.

4. Spray a large pan with cooking spray and heat over medium-high heat. Fry the patties for 8 minutes on each side, or until firm and golden.

15. Veggie Patties with Tofu and Plantain Medley

15-minute prep time Time to prepare: 10 minutes Time allotted: 25 minutes 5 servings

Ingredients

• 14 cup cubed tofu • 14 cup chopped zucchini • 1 peeled and sliced plantain • 12 cup canned sliced mushrooms • 12 cup sun-dried tomatoes • 12 cup bread crumbs • 14 cup black olives • 1 big garlic bulb, coarsely chopped

• 1 tablespoon butter (or more if necessary)

Directions

1. In a blender, combine tofu, zucchini, plantain, mushrooms, sun-dried tomatoes, bread crumbs, olives, and garlic until a uniform, thick texture is achieved. Spoon the mixture into your hand and form patties with it.

2. Melt butter in a cast iron skillet over medium heat; brown patties in the hot butter, pressing lightly with a spatula, 3 to 5 minutes per side.

Burgers with Sweet Potato and Black Beans, No. 16

Time to Prepare: 25 minutes Time to prepare: 51 minutes 1 hr 16 mins total time

6 servings

Ingredients

• 1 large sweet potato • 1 cooking spray • 2 (15 ounce) cans rinsed and drained black beans • 12 cup quick cooking oats • 14 cup chopped onion • 1 tablespoon Dijon mustard • 1 teaspoon ground cumin • 14 teaspoon freshly grated ginger • 14 teaspoon salt

Directions

1. Preheat the oven to 400 degrees Fahrenheit (200 degrees C). With a fork, poke a few holes in the sweet potato and place on a greased baking sheet.

2. Bake in a preheated oven for 35 to 45 minutes, or until sweet potatoes are easily pierced with a fork. Remove from the oven and set aside to cool until you can handle it. Reduce the heat to 350 degrees Fahrenheit (175 degrees C). Using cooking spray, coat a baking sheet.

3. Peel the sweet potato and place it in a big mixing bowl. Mash the black beans with a fork or a whisk. Combine the oats, onions,

Dijon mustard, cumin, ginger, salt, and cinnamon in a mixing bowl. With wet hands, form the mixture into 6 patties and place on the prepared baking sheet.

4. Bake for 8 minutes on each side in a preheated oven until cooked in the center and crisp on the outside.

Time to prepare the lasagna: 30 minutes

Time to cook: 2 hours and 30 minutes

3 hrs 15 mins total time

12 servings

Ingredients

• 8 ounces chopped plant-based hot Italian-style sausage (such as Beyond Meat) • 6 ounces cooked and crumbled ground meat substitute (such as BOCA) • 1 (15 ounce) can crushed tomatoes • 1 (8 ounce) can tomato sauce • 1 (6 ounce) can tomato paste • 14 cup water

• 3 tablespoons chopped fresh parsley, divided • 1 tablespoon white sugar • 34 teaspoon dried basil • 1 teaspoon salt, divided • 12 teaspoon Italian seasoning • 14 teaspoon fennel seeds • 18 teaspoon ground black pepper • 12 lasagna noodles • 1 egg, lightly beaten

Directions

1. In a Dutch oven, heat the oil over medium heat. Cook, stirring occasionally, until the onion and garlic are tender, 3 to 5 minutes.

2. Combine the plant-based sausage, meat substitute crumbles, crushed tomatoes, tomato sauce, tomato paste, water, 1 tablespoon parsley, sugar, basil, 1/2 teaspoon salt, Italian seasoning, fennel seeds, and pepper in a large mixing bowl.

3. Bring to a boil; reduce heat to low and cook, covered, for 1 1/2 hours, stirring occasionally.

4. Bring a large pot of water to a boil, lightly salted. Cook for 8 to 10 minutes after adding the lasagna noodles. Using cold water, drain and rinse the noodles.

5. Preheat the oven to 375°F (190°C) (190 degrees C).

6. In a separate bowl, whisk together the egg, ricotta, remaining 2 tablespoons parsley, and 1/2 teaspoon salt.

7. To assemble the lasagna, in a 9x13-inch baking dish, spread 1/3 of the sauce. Place 6 noodles lengthwise on top of the sauce. 1/2 of the ricotta should be spread on top.

mixture. 1/3 of the mozzarella slices should be on top. 1/3 of the sauce should be poured over the mozzarella, and 1/4 cup Parmesan should be sprinkled on top.

8. Continue layering with the remaining mozzarella and Parmesan.

9. Bake for 25 minutes, covered with cooking spray-coated foil. Remove the foil and bake for another 25 minutes, or until hot and bubbly. Allow to cool for 15 minutes before slicing into 12 portions.

Curry with sweet potatoes, spinach, and halloumi

Time to prepare: 20 minutes Time to prepare: 35 minutes Time allotted: 55 minutes 4 Servings

Ingredients

• 2 large peeled and chopped sweet potatoes • 1 (14.5 oz) can diced tomatoes • 3 teaspoons curry powder • 2 teaspoons chili powder • 1 teaspoon ground cumin • 1 (14.5 oz) can coconut milk

• 1 package fresh spinach (8 ounces) • 12 diced green chile pepper, or to taste • 1 cube vegetable bouillon • 2 teaspoons chili jam (Optional)

• 1 (8.8 ounce) package sliced halloumi cheese

• 1 can chickpeas (14 ounces), drained Directions

1. Place sweet potatoes in a large pot with enough water to cover them and bring to a boil. Cook for about 6 minutes, or until the vegetables are tender. Drain.

2. In a medium saucepan, combine sweet potatoes, tomatoes, curry powder, chili powder, and cumin and bring to a simmer.

3. Combine the coconut milk, spinach, chile pepper, bouillon cube, and chili jam in a large mixing bowl. Cook for 15 to 20 minutes, or until the curry has thickened and cooked down a little.

4. Meanwhile, in a skillet over medium heat, brown halloumi for 4 to 6 minutes. Heat through the cooked halloumi and chickpeas in the curry, about 5 minutes.

Pancakes with a Rainbow of Colors

Time to Prepare: 15 minutes Time to cook: 10 minutes Time allotted: 25 mins 14 servings

Russet Pancakes Ingredients: 3 cups grated russet potatoes, 3 tablespoons grated yellow onion, 12 teaspoons kosher salt, 5 tablespoons potato starch, 2 eggs, beaten, 18 teaspoon ground white pepper, 1 cup vegetable oil for frying, or more as needed

Pancakes in Purple:

• 4 cups grated purple potatoes • 3 tablespoons grated red onion • 12 teaspoon kosher salt • 5 tablespoons potato starch • 2 eggs, beaten • 18 teaspoon ground black pepper • 1 teaspoon balsamic vinegar

Directions

1. Preheat the vegetable oil in a skillet until it reaches 350 degrees F for the russet pancakes.

2. Peel and grate the potatoes and onion, then set them aside. Fill a clean bar towel or cloth with the measured amounts. Squeeze out as much water as you can.

3. In a separate bowl, whisk together the eggs, potato starch, salt, and white pepper until smooth. Fold the onion and potatoes into the egg mixture quickly.

4. To portion out a potato pancake, use a 1/4 cup measuring cup. Using a spatula, flatten the dough into the hot oil.

5. Fry until golden brown, flipping with a slotted spatula halfway through (about 4 minutes per side). Cook for another minute or two until the second side is golden brown.

6. Transfer the pancake to a drain pan or rack using a slotted spatula. Season with kosher salt.

7. Using the same ingredients as the purple potato pancakes, follow the same directions.

20. Mushroom Soup with Coconut-Tamari

Time to Prepare: 10 minutes 45 minutes to prepare 1 hr 15 mins total time

8 Servings

Ingredients

• 2 cubes vegetable bouillon • 6 cups boiling water • 4 cups sliced fresh mushrooms • 3 tablespoons dried wakame (brown) seaweed • 3 tablespoons olive oil • 3 garlic cloves, minced • 2 cans coconut milk (14 ounces)

• 1 teaspoon tamari, or to taste • 14 cup chopped fresh cilantro • 1 lime, juiced

Directions

1. Boil the water and dissolve the vegetable bouillon cubes, then add the sliced mushrooms and set aside for 20 minutes.

2. In a small bowl, cover the seaweed with warm water and set aside.

3. In a large saucepan, heat the olive oil over medium-low heat. Cook, stirring frequently, until the garlic has softened, about 5 minutes. Remove the mushrooms from the vegetable broth and squeeze out any excess liquid; set aside the broth.

4. Add the mushrooms to the pot and cook, stirring occasionally, until they have browned and are tender, about 15 minutes. Pour in the coconut milk and the vegetable broth that was set aside.

5. Squeeze out any excess water from the wakame. Toss the wakame with the cilantro, lime juice, and tamari in the pot. Bring to a boil over high heat, then reduce to medium-low heat, cover, and keep warm.

and cook for about 20 minutes to allow the flavors to mingle.

21. Green Chile Cilantro Quinoa Bowl with Vegan Mexican Quinoa

30 minute prep time Time to cook: 20 minutes Time allotted: 50 minutes 4 Servings

Ingredients

Green Chile Cilantro Sauce (Vegan):

• 1 cup unsalted raw cashews • 1 (4 oz) chopped green chile peppers • 14 cup hemp milk • 12 jalapeno pepper with seeds, or more to taste • 12 teaspoon salt • 1 14 cup chopped fresh cilantro • 3 cups water • 1 12 cup quinoa

• 2 (15 ounce) rinsed and drained black bean cans • 3 cups chopped red bell pepper • 12 cup chopped red onion • 2 avocados, chopped

Directions

1. In a blender, puree the cashews, green chile peppers, hemp milk, jalapeno pepper, and salt until smooth.

2. Transfer the cashew mixture to a small bowl and stir in 1 cup cilantro. 3. Bring the cashew mixture to a boil in a saucepan. Reduce heat to medium-low, cover, and cook for 15 to 20 minutes, or until quinoa is tender.

3. Divide the romaine lettuce between four bowls. Quinoa, black beans, red bell pepper, and onion go on top.

4. Finish with a drizzle of cilantro sauce. Serve with the remaining 1/4 cup cilantro and chopped avocados as a garnish.

Ginataang Manok (number 22) (Chicken Cooked in Coconut Milk)

Prep Time: 10 mins 1 hour and 5 minutes to prepare

Total Time: 1 hr 15 mins

Servings: 6

Ingredients

2 (14 ounce) cans coconut milk • 1 (10 ounce) package frozen chopped spinach, thawed and drained • 3 tablespoons canola oil • 12 cup sliced fresh ginger • 1 (5 pound) whole chicken, cut into pieces • salt and ground black pepper to taste

Directions

1. In a large skillet, heat the canola oil over medium heat and add the ginger slices. Cook, stirring constantly, until the mixture is fragrant and lightly browned. Take out the ginger and set it aside. Season the chicken with salt and pepper before serving.

2. Cook the chicken in the same skillet over medium-high heat, making sure it doesn't overcrowd. Cook until all sides of the chicken are lightly browned.

3. Add the coconut milk to the skillet with the ginger. Bring to a boil, then remove from heat and tilt the lid to allow steam to escape.

4. Reduce heat to medium-low and cook, stirring occasionally, until the chicken is no longer pink at the bone, about 30 minutes.

5. Add the spinach and mix well. Cook, uncovered, for 8 to 12 minutes, or until spinach is warmed through. As needed, season with salt and pepper.

Sotanghon de Pollo de Pollo de Pollo de Pollo de Pollo de Poll

Prep Time: 25 mins Time to prepare: 30 minutes 1 hr 25 mins total time

10 servings

Ingredients

• 3 tablespoons olive oil • 1 onion, chopped • 2 garlic cloves, minced • 12 teaspoons achiote powder • 1 tablespoon fish sauce • 2 cups water • 1 teaspoon salt • 1 pound chicken legs • 1 ounce dried shiitake mushrooms • 8 ounces bean thread noodles (cellophane noodles)

• season with salt and pepper to taste

• 2 cans (14.5 oz.) chicken broth

• 2 chopped green onions

Directions

1. In a pot, bring 2 cups water and 1 teaspoon salt to a boil; cook the chicken in the boiling water for 10 minutes, or until no longer pink in the center and the juices run clear.

2. Insert an instant-read thermometer into the center and check for a temperature of at least 165 degrees F. (74 degrees C). Remove the chicken from the pan and set aside the liquid before removing the meat from the bones and shredding with two forks. Remove the skin and bones and toss them out.

3. While the chicken cools, place the shiitake mushrooms in a bowl and cover with enough warm water to cover completely; soak for 30 minutes or until pliable. Take the fish out of the water, slice it, and set it aside.

4. Place the bean thread noodles in the water and cover with more warm water if necessary; soak for 10 minutes or until soft. Drain. If desired, cut the noodles.

5. In a skillet over medium heat, heat the olive oil; cook and stir the onion and garlic until softened, about 5 minutes. Continue to cook and stir in the achiote powder until the mixture is well coated in the red-orange color.

6. Season with salt and pepper to taste and stir in the shredded chicken meat, sliced shiitake mushrooms, and fish sauce.

7. Cook for about 5 minutes before adding the chicken broth and the reserved liquid from the chicken.

8. Cook for 5 minutes after bringing to a boil. Cook for another 5 minutes after adding the noodles. To serve, garnish with green onion.

Afritad de Pollo de Pollo de Pollo de Pollo de Pollo de Pollo de Pollo de Poll

Prep Time: 10 mins 3 HOURS TO COOK

3 hours and 20 minutes total

Servings: 6

Ingredients

• 12 cup soy sauce, or to taste • 12 cup olive oil, or to taste • 1 lemon, juiced • 3 garlic cloves, minced • pounded black pepper to taste • 2 tomatoes, diced • 2 carrots, chopped • 3 red potatoes, cubed • 1 onion, sliced (Optional)

• 1 cup green peas • 1 green bell pepper, sliced Directions

1. In a slow cooker, marinate the chicken, soy sauce, olive oil, lemon juice, garlic, and black pepper for 10 to 15 minutes.

2. In a large mixing bowl, combine the tomatoes, carrots, red potatoes, onion, green bell pepper, red bell pepper, yellow bell pepper, and peas.

3. Cook for 3 to 4 hours on high on the stove (or on Low for 7 to 8 hours).

Caldo de Pollo de Pollo de Pollo de Pollo de Pollo de Pollo de Poll (Chicken Rice Porridge)

20-Minute Preparation 30 Minutes to Prepare 50 minutes total 5 people

Ingredients

• 2 tablespoons olive oil • 1 onion, diced • 2 garlic cloves, crushed

• 1 (2 inch) piece fresh ginger, peeled and thinly sliced • 14 pound chicken wings, split and tips discarded (Optional)

1 cup glutinous sweet rice • salt and pepper to taste • 1 chopped green onion

1 sliced lemon (Optional)

• if desired, 1 teaspoon fish sauce to sprinkling (Optional)

Directions

1. In a large pot over medium heat, heat the olive oil; cook and stir the onion, garlic, and ginger for about 5 minutes, or until fragrant.

2. Cook and stir for 1 minute after adding the chicken wings. Cook for an additional 2 minutes after adding the fish sauce to the pot.

3. Fill the pot with the chicken broth. In a separate bowl, combine the sweet rice and stir until well combined.

4. Bring the mixture to a boil, then cover and cook for 10 minutes, stirring occasionally to keep the rice from sticking to the bottom of the pan. Using salt and pepper, season to taste.

5. Serve with lemon slices and more fish sauce, if desired.

Prep Time: 20 minutes for Authentic Chicken Adobo 1 hr 30 mins to prepare

5 hours and 50 minutes total

8 people

Ingredients

12 cup soy sauce • 2 cups coconut vinegar

10 bay leaves • 1 tablespoon garlic powder • 1 head garlic, peeled

and coarsely chopped

• 12 teaspoons annatto powder • 12 teaspoons ground black pepper

• Cut-up chicken parts, 5 12 pound

• 1 garlic head, peeled and coarsely chopped • 12 teaspoons

annatto powder

Directions

1. In a large mixing bowl, whisk together the vinegar, soy sauce, 1

garlic head, bay leaves, garlic powder, black pepper, and 1 1/2 teaspoons annatto powder. Cover and refrigerate for at least 4 hours after adding the chicken.

2. Pat chicken dry after removing it from the marinade. The marinade should be kept separate.

3. In a large skillet over medium-high heat, heat 2 tablespoons vegetable oil Cook the chicken for 4 minutes per side in the hot oil. Turn off the stovetop.

In a small skillet over medium heat, heat 1 tablespoon vegetable oil. 3 minutes of stirring and cooking 1 head garlic Simmer for 3 minutes with 1 1/2 teaspoon annatto powder.

5. Toss the chicken with the annatto mixture and the marinade that was set aside. Bring to a low boil, cover, and cook for 45 minutes, or until chicken is tender.

6. Remove the lid and cook for about 10 minutes, or until the sauce has slightly reduced.

27. Pancit Quick & Easy

20-Minute Preparation 20-minute cooking time 40 minutes total 6 people

Ingredients

• 1 cup diced cooked chicken breast meat • 1 small head cabbage, thinly sliced • 4 carrot, thinly sliced • 14 cup soy sauce

• 2 lemon wedges (for garnish)

Directions

1. Fill a large bowl halfway with warm water and add the rice noodles. Drain and set aside when the potatoes have become soft.

2. In a large skillet or wok, heat the oil over medium heat. Cook onion and garlic in a skillet until they are soft. Combine the chicken, cabbage, carrots, and soy sauce in a large mixing bowl.

3. Continue to cook until the cabbage softens. Cook, stirring constantly, until the noodles are heated through.

4. Serve pancit with quartered lemons on top.

Adobo Chicken with Bok Choy in a Slow Cooker

10 Minutes to Prepare 8 hrs 5 mins to cook

8 hours and 15 minutes total

4 people

Ingredients

• 2 onions, sliced • 4 garlic cloves, smashed • 2/3 cup apple cider vinegar • 1/3 cup soy sauce • 1 tablespoon brown sugar • 1 bay leaf

• 1 bok choy head, sliced into 1-inch strips

2 thinly sliced green onions

Directions

1. In a slow cooker, mix together the onions, garlic, apple cider vinegar, soy sauce, brown sugar, and bay leaf. Black pepper is a good addition.

2. Top with chicken thighs. Season chicken thighs with paprika.

3. Cook for 8 hours on low, covered.

4. Increase the temperature of the slow cooker to high. Cook another 5 minutes after adding the bok choy to the chicken mixture. Add green onions as a garnish.

29. Bringhe

30 Minutes Preparation 40-minute cooking time 1 hour and 10 minutes (total)

10 portions

Ingredients

1 onion, chopped • 2 garlic cloves, minced • 1 teaspoon curry powder

12 pound peeled and deveined tiger prawns • 12 pound cubed fully cooked ham • 2 bay leaves • salt and pepper to taste

• 1 coconut milk (16 ounce) can

1 c. glutinous white rice, uncooked Directions

1. In a large skillet over medium heat, heat the olive oil and cook and stir the onion and garlic until translucent, about 5 to 7 minutes. Stir in the curry powder to evenly coat the chicken.

2. Stir in the chicken. Cook for 2 minutes covered in the skillet. Cook for another 2 minutes after adding the prawns to the mix.

3. Mix in the ham and bay leaves, seasoning with salt and pepper. Cook for an additional 2 minutes with the skillet covered.

4. Add the coconut milk to the skillet and stir to combine. Stir in the rice. Reduce heat to low and cover; cook for 30 minutes, stirring occasionally. Warm it up and serve.

30. Adobo de Pollo de Pollo de Pollo de Pollo de Pollo de Pollo de Pollo

15-Minute Preparation 35-minute cooking time 50 minutes total 8 people

Ingredients

• 3 pounds skinless, boneless chicken thighs • 12 cup soy sauce •
12 cup water • 34 cup vinegar • 3 tablespoons honey

Directions

1. Lightly oil the grate of an outdoor grill and heat it to high.

2. Mix soy sauce, water, vinegar, honey, garlic, bay leaves, and pepper in a large pot.

3. Bring the liquid to a boil, then add the chicken. Reduce the heat to low and cook for 35 to 40 minutes, covered.

4. Remove the chicken from the pan and drain it on paper towels. Bay leaves should be thrown out. Bring the mixture back to a boil, then reduce to 1 1/2 cup.

5. Cook the chicken for 5 minutes on each side on a preheated grill, or until browned and crisp. Serve the rest of the soy sauce mixture on the side.Ingredients

• 12 cup soy sauce, or to taste • 12 cup olive oil, or to taste • 1 lemon, juiced • 3 garlic cloves, minced • pounded black pepper to taste • 2 tomatoes, diced • 2 carrots, chopped • 3 red potatoes, cubed • 1 onion, sliced (Optional)

• 1 cup green peas • 1 green bell pepper, sliced Directions

1. In a slow cooker, marinate the chicken, soy sauce, olive oil, lemon juice, garlic, and black pepper for 10 to 15 minutes.

2. In a large mixing bowl, combine the tomatoes, carrots, red potatoes, onion, green bell pepper, red bell pepper, yellow bell pepper, and peas.

3. Cook for 3 to 4 hours on high on the stove (or on Low for 7 to 8 hours).

Caldo de Pollo de Pollo de Pollo de Pollo de Pollo de Pollo de Poll (Chicken Rice Porridge)

20-Minute Preparation 30 Minutes to Prepare 50 minutes total 5 people

Ingredients

• 2 tablespoons olive oil • 1 onion, diced • 2 garlic cloves, crushed

• 1 (2 inch) piece fresh ginger, peeled and thinly sliced • 14 pound chicken wings, split and tips discarded (Optional)

1 cup glutinous sweet rice • salt and pepper to taste • 1 chopped green onion

1 sliced lemon (Optional)

• if desired, 1 teaspoon fish sauce to sprinkling (Optional)

Directions

1. In a large pot over medium heat, heat the olive oil; cook and stir the onion, garlic, and ginger for about 5 minutes, or until fragrant.

2. Cook and stir for 1 minute after adding the chicken wings. Cook for an additional 2 minutes after adding the fish sauce to the pot.

3. Fill the pot with the chicken broth. In a separate bowl, combine the sweet rice and stir until well combined.

4. Bring the mixture to a boil, then cover and cook for 10 minutes, stirring occasionally to keep the rice from sticking to the bottom of the pan. Using salt and pepper, season to taste.

5. Serve with lemon slices and more fish sauce, if desired.

Prep Time: 20 minutes for Authentic Chicken Adobo 1 hr 30 mins to prepare

5 hours and 50 minutes total

8 people

Ingredients

12 cup soy sauce • 2 cups coconut vinegar

10 bay leaves • 1 tablespoon garlic powder • 1 head garlic, peeled and coarsely chopped

• 12 teaspoons annatto powder • 12 teaspoons ground black pepper

• Cut-up chicken parts, 5 12 pound

• 1 garlic head, peeled and coarsely chopped • 12 teaspoons annatto powder

Directions

1. In a large mixing bowl, whisk together the vinegar, soy sauce, 1 garlic head, bay leaves, garlic powder, black pepper, and 1 1/2

teaspoons annatto powder. Cover and refrigerate for at least 4 hours after adding the chicken.

2. Pat chicken dry after removing it from the marinade. The marinade should be kept separate.

3. In a large skillet over medium-high heat, heat 2 tablespoons vegetable oil Cook the chicken for 4 minutes per side in the hot oil. Turn off the stovetop.

In a small skillet over medium heat, heat 1 tablespoon vegetable oil. 3 minutes of stirring and cooking 1 head garlic Simmer for 3 minutes with 1 1/2 teaspoon annatto powder.

5. Toss the chicken with the annatto mixture and the marinade that was set aside. Bring to a low boil, cover, and cook for 45 minutes, or until chicken is tender.

6. Remove the lid and cook for about 10 minutes, or until the sauce has slightly reduced.

27. Pancit Quick & Easy

20-Minute Preparation 20-minute cooking time 40 minutes total 6 people

Ingredients

• 1 cup diced cooked chicken breast meat • 1 small head cabbage, thinly sliced • 4 carrot, thinly sliced • 14 cup soy sauce

• 2 lemon wedges (for garnish)

Directions

1. Fill a large bowl halfway with warm water and add the rice noodles. Drain and set aside when the potatoes have become soft.

2. In a large skillet or wok, heat the oil over medium heat. Cook onion and garlic in a skillet until they are soft. Combine the chicken, cabbage, carrots, and soy sauce in a large mixing bowl.

3. Continue to cook until the cabbage softens. Cook, stirring constantly, until the noodles are heated through.

4. Serve pancit with quartered lemons on top.

Adobo Chicken with Bok Choy in a Slow Cooker

10 Minutes to Prepare 8 hrs 5 mins to cook

8 hours and 15 minutes total

4 people

Ingredients

• 2 onions, sliced • 4 garlic cloves, smashed • 2/3 cup apple cider vinegar • 1/3 cup soy sauce • 1 tablespoon brown sugar • 1 bay leaf

• 1 bok choy head, sliced into 1-inch strips

2 thinly sliced green onions

Directions

1. In a slow cooker, mix together the onions, garlic, apple cider vinegar, soy sauce, brown sugar, and bay leaf. Black pepper is a good addition.

2. Top with chicken thighs. Season chicken thighs with paprika.

3. Cook for 8 hours on low, covered.

4. Increase the temperature of the slow cooker to high. Cook another 5 minutes after adding the bok choy to the chicken mixture. Add green onions as a garnish.

29. Bringhe

30 Minutes Preparation 40-minute cooking time 1 hour and 10 minutes (total)

10 portions

Ingredients

1 onion, chopped • 2 garlic cloves, minced • 1 teaspoon curry powder

12 pound peeled and deveined tiger prawns • 12 pound cubed fully cooked ham • 2 bay leaves • salt and pepper to taste

• 1 coconut milk (16 ounce) can

1 c. glutinous white rice, uncooked Directions

1. In a large skillet over medium heat, heat the olive oil and cook and stir the onion and garlic until translucent, about 5 to 7 minutes. Stir in the curry powder to evenly coat the chicken.

2. Stir in the chicken. Cook for 2 minutes covered in the skillet. Cook for another 2 minutes after adding the prawns to the mix.

3. Mix in the ham and bay leaves, seasoning with salt and pepper. Cook for an additional 2 minutes with the skillet covered.

4. Add the coconut milk to the skillet and stir to combine. Stir in the rice. Reduce heat to low and cover; cook for 30 minutes, stirring occasionally. Warm it up and serve.

30. Adobo de Pollo de Pollo de Pollo de Pollo de Pollo de Pollo de Pollo

15-Minute Preparation 35-minute cooking time 50 minutes total 8 people

Ingredients

• 3 pounds skinless, boneless chicken thighs • 12 cup soy sauce •
12 cup water • 34 cup vinegar • 3 tablespoons honey

Directions

1. Lightly oil the grate of an outdoor grill and heat it to high.

2. Mix soy sauce, water, vinegar, honey, garlic, bay leaves, and pepper in a large pot.

3. Bring the liquid to a boil, then add the chicken. Reduce the heat to low and cook for 35 to 40 minutes, covered.

4. Remove the chicken from the pan and drain it on paper towels. Bay leaves should be thrown out. Bring the mixture back to a boil, then reduce to 1 1/2 cup.

5. Cook the chicken for 5 minutes on each side on a preheated grill, or until browned and crisp. Serve the rest of the soy sauce mixture on the side.

The Basis of Cardiac Diet

Red Meat
Monthly or small amounts

Sweets
A few times per month

Eggs
A few times per week

Poultry
A few times per week

Fish
A few times per week

Cheese & Yogurt
Daily Servings

Olive Oil
In variable amounts

Fruit
Daily Servings

Vegetables
Daily Servings

Beans, Legumes, & Nuts
Daily Servings

Bread, Pasta, Rice,
Couscous, Polenta,
Other Grains, & Potatoes
Daily Servings

Daily Physical Activity

Mediterranean Diet Pyramid